Cones of Ice Crème

A book by RL Lane

"You missed the ice creaM", she told me. I listened to her story. It was a funny one. It is true, I had missed the ice cream, but I didn't miss her story. My Mom's." RL Lane

Introduction: It is Memorial Day. 2015.

It seemed like the write day to right the way

For you to see…

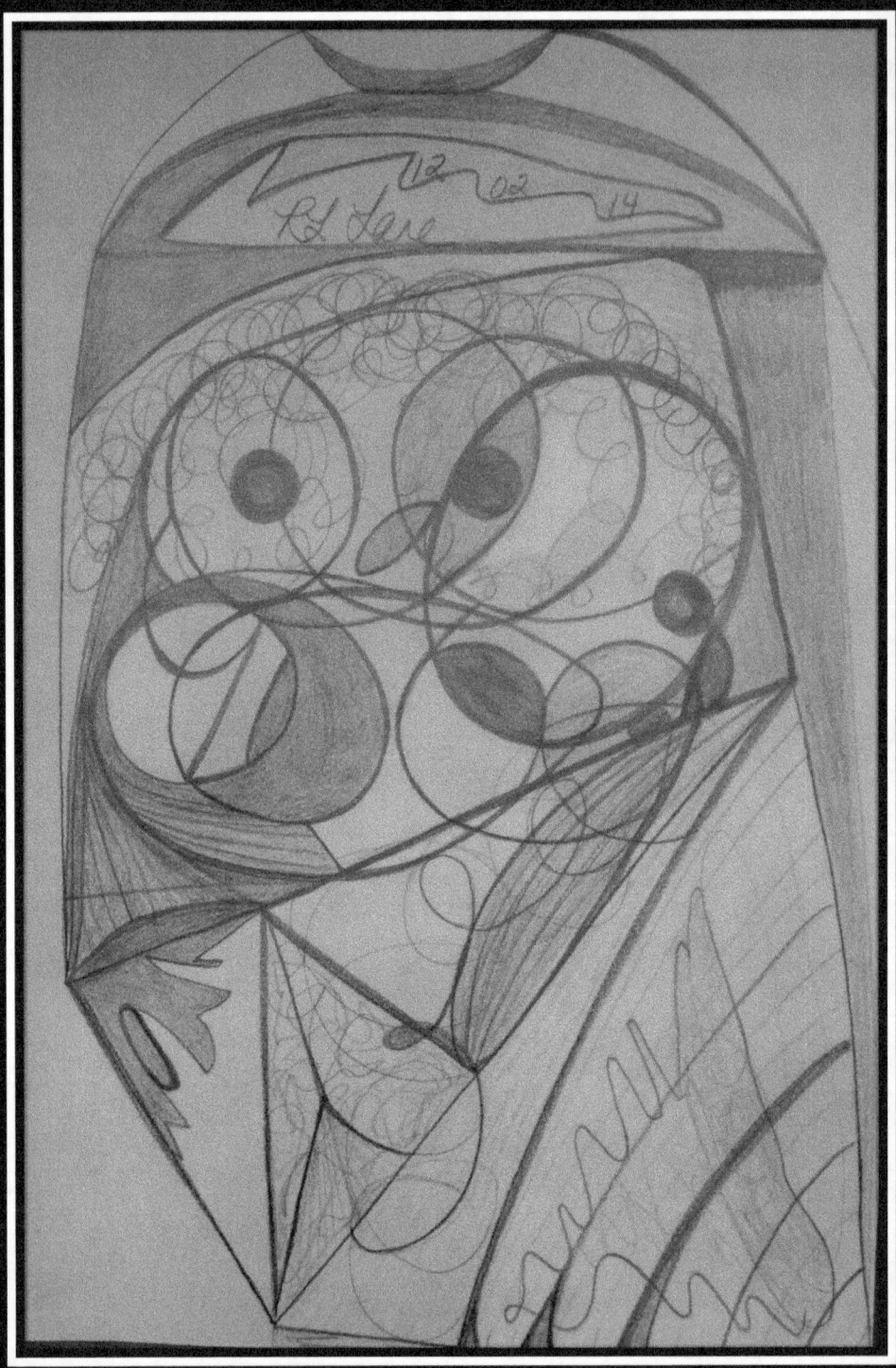

We can look through a lens or just through our eyes. We can look this way…to see her walking under the archway in her wedding dress after she makes it over the mountain of rough peaks…

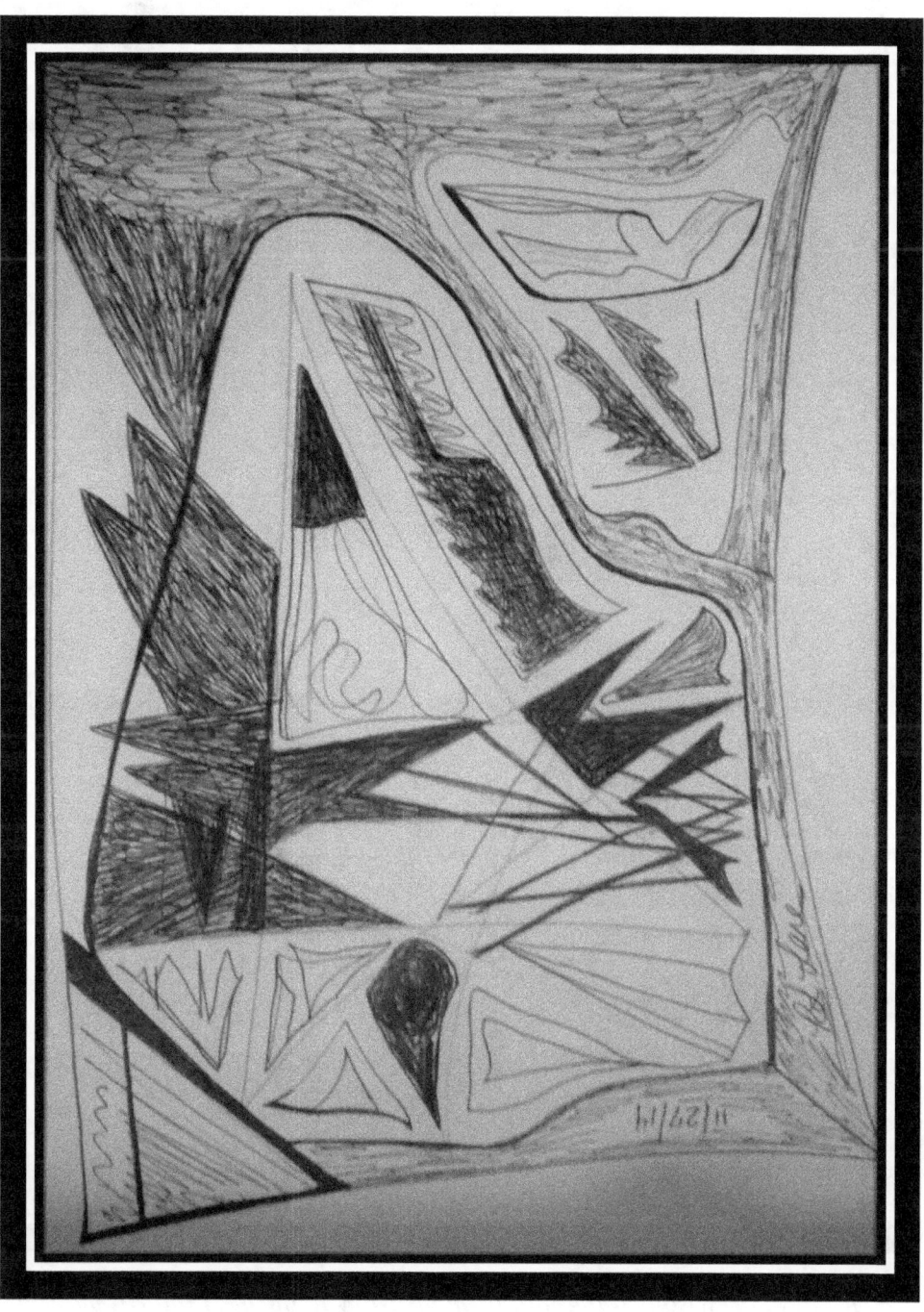

Or we can look this way and just see the mask…

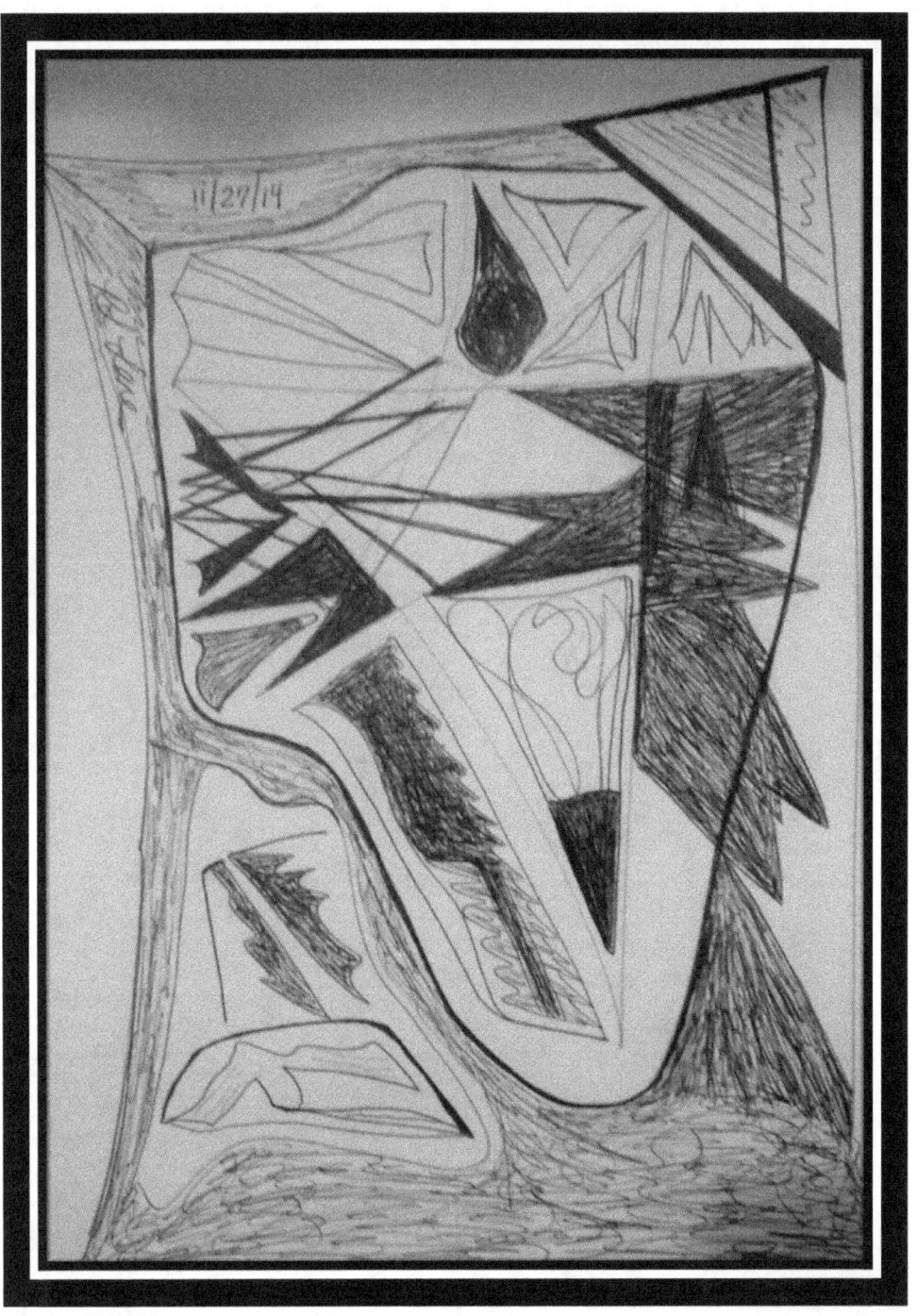

He says I drew something that is on his Navy uniform. I think it may be the drawings in the lower left-hand corner…

I called this "Pinball Hearts", but it was never a game…

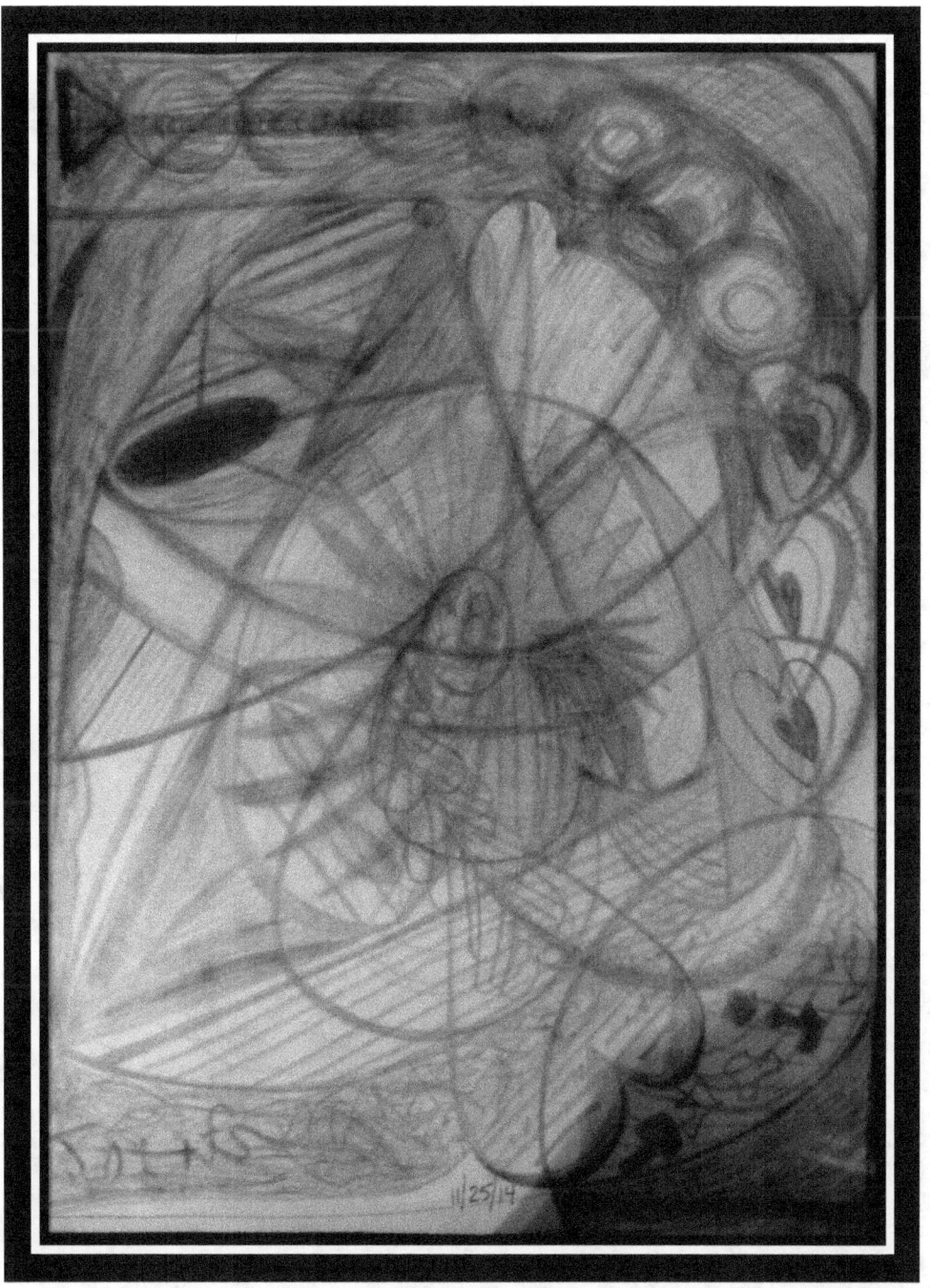

You should never push around someone's heart…

Everyone needs help every now and then. You can't climb a mountain with scuba gear. You can't fly a kite in the water. *Or can you? Tie it to the end of your boat and let it fly away…*

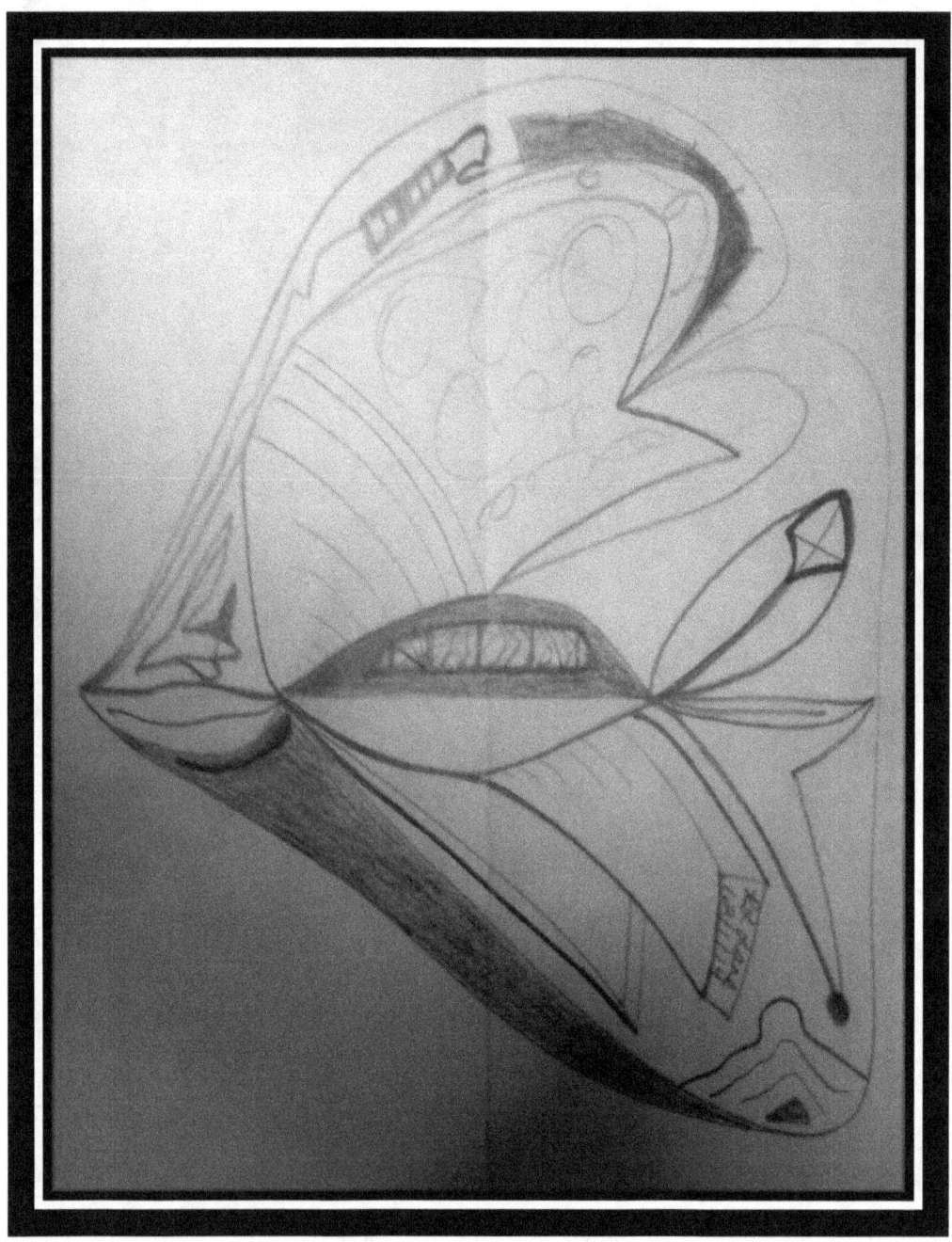

Or is that bird-like drawing in the fish's face the thing that is on his Navy uniform?

I called this "Brown Eye and Mr. Wig". It is still one of my favorite stories. Oh. You already saw this. Did you see the sailboat? Do you see the one eye? Do you see the Wig? *Did Pirates wear wigs?*

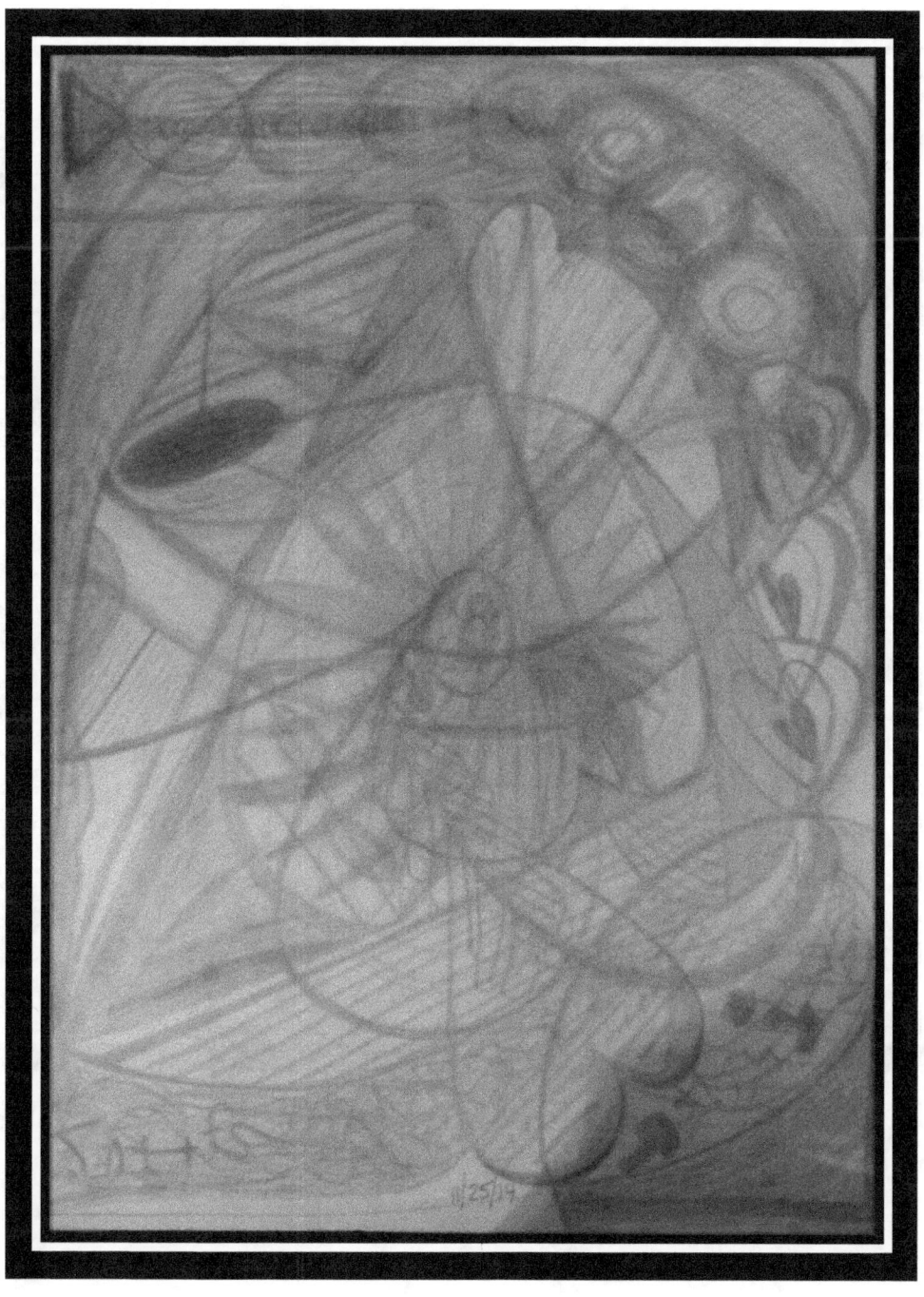

He was on a boat most of the time. USS LST 494. But he was also on a plane. I hope it wasn't hit while he was serving our country. *I don't think this plane had food service…*

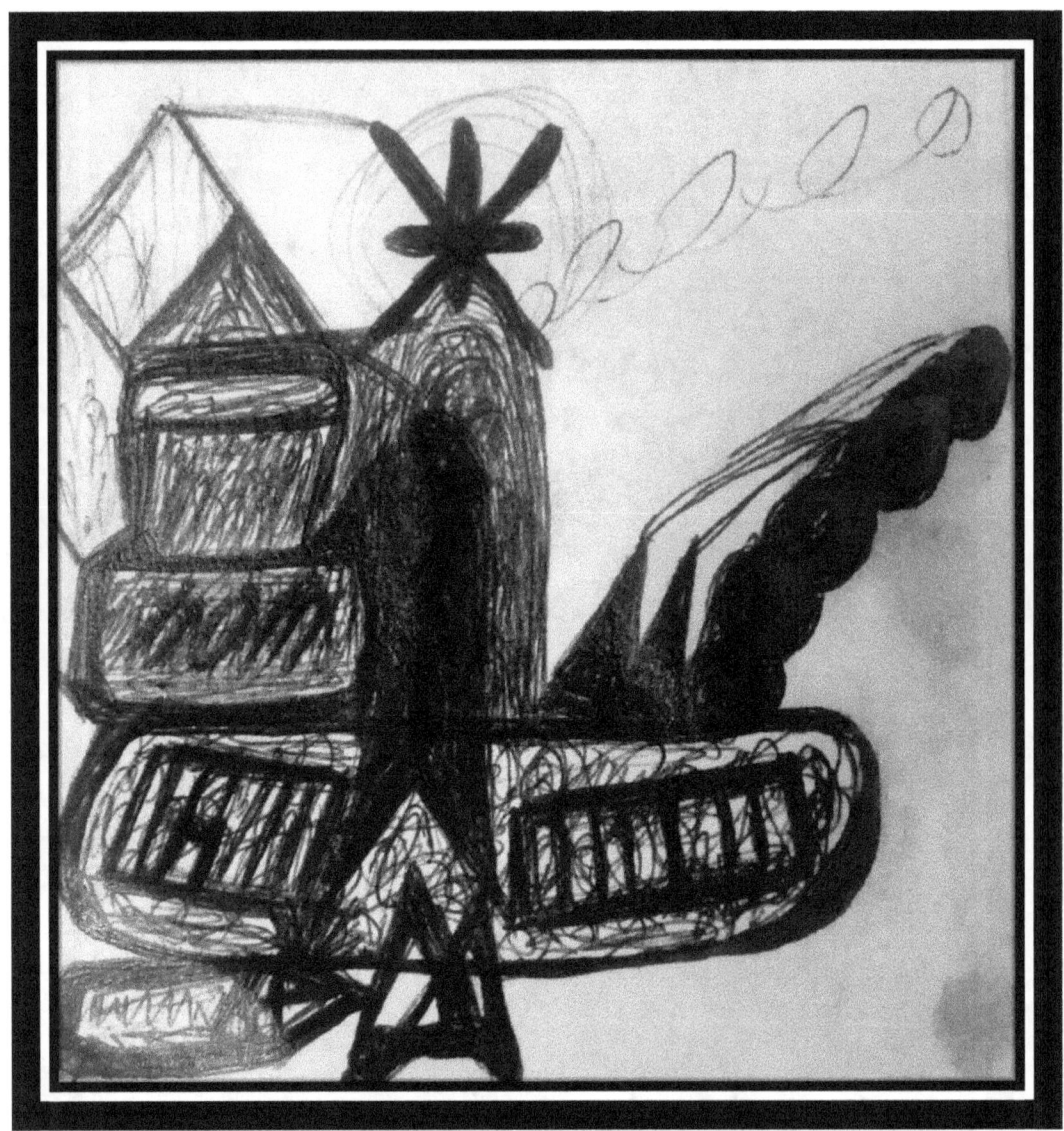

There is something important about the front of the plane. The shapes that look like triangles. My brain keeps thinking about oil drills…

This one is pretty. To me it is pretty. The lily. The flag. A monument. Things to remember the Mom and the Dad and the Doctor…and things they loved to do…

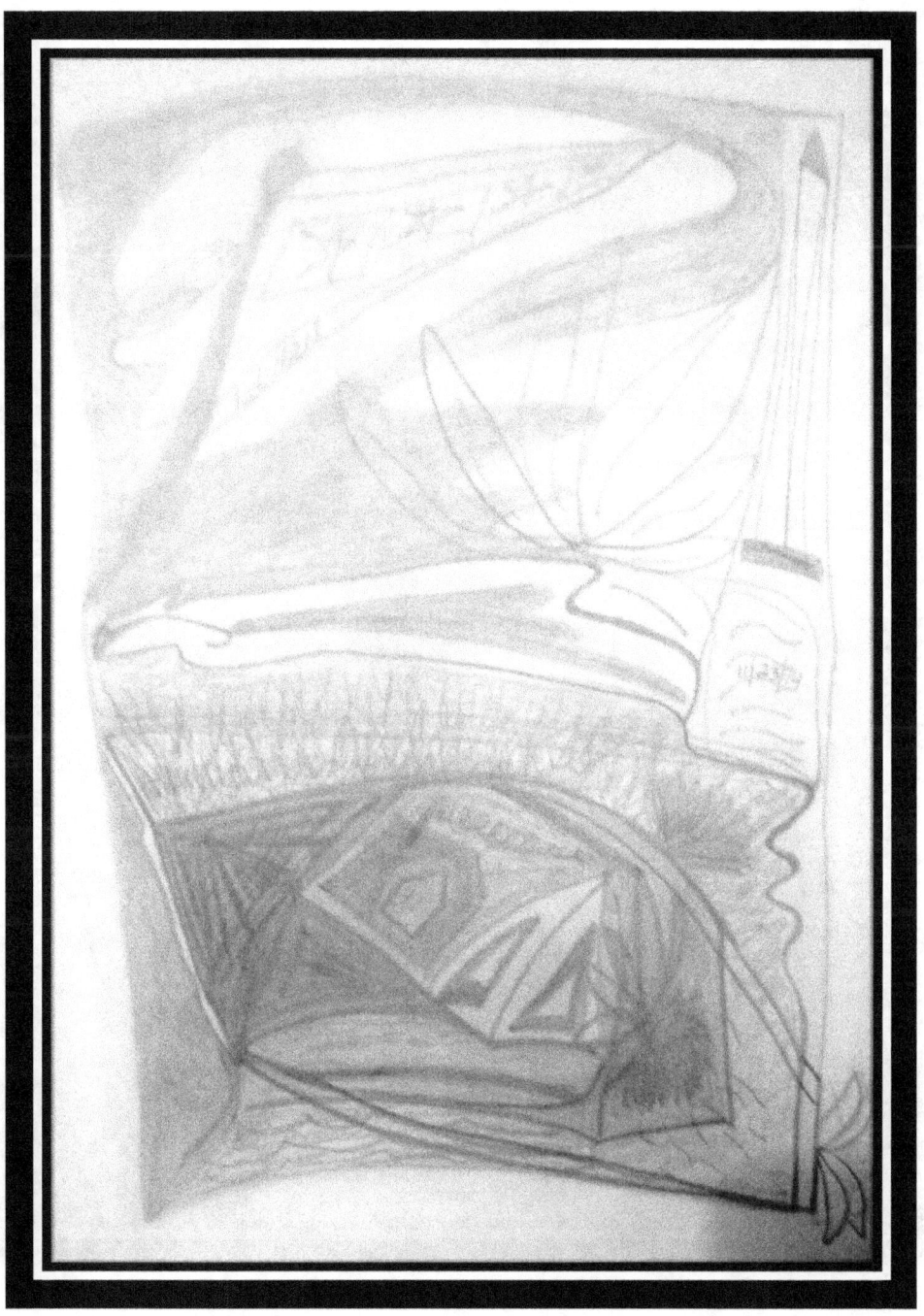

Which monument did I draw? Does anyone recognize it?

Oh, the old hobo man. The one who rode the rails. Do you see him walking around lost in the middle of the tracks? *He tells one of my favorite stories…*

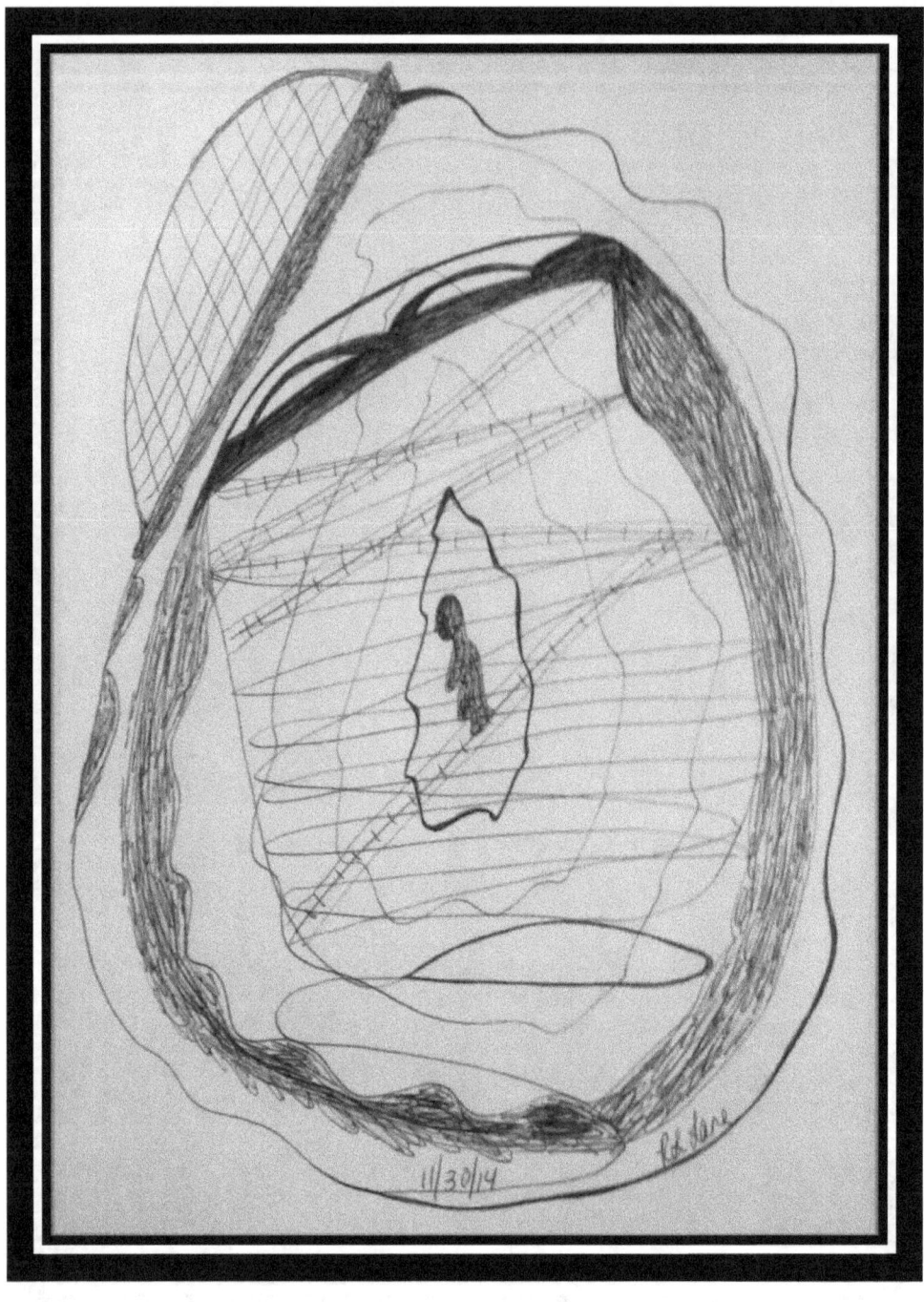

Have you figured it out yet? These drawings are…

The "tree of life" has one side dead and one side alive. Inside it there are 2 ghosts. One is holding a book. Is the one holding the book on the live side because she is alive? He is on the dead side because he is already dead. The Doctor is already dead…

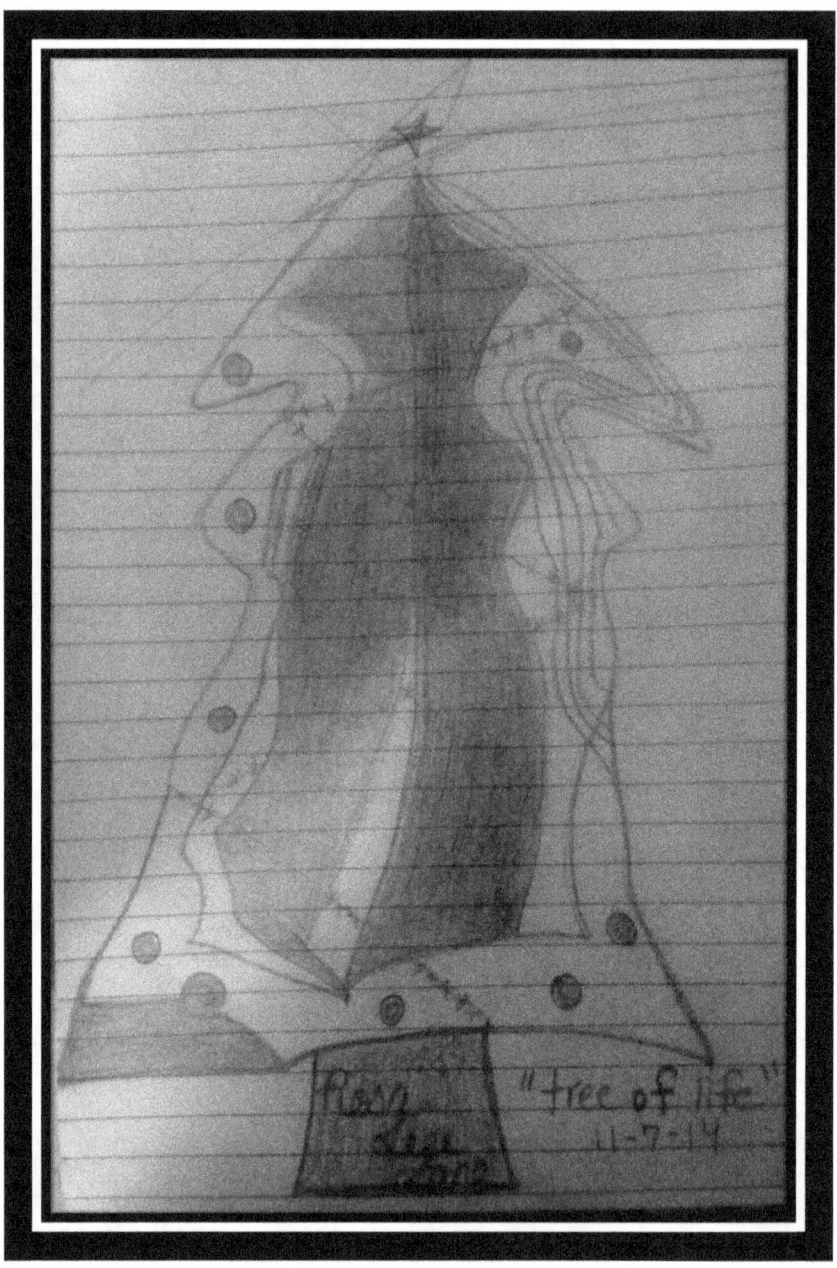

There is a bell upside-down in the lower left-hand corner. Light is shooting up from the bell…

"All aboard", the conductor would yell and the bell would clang. The trains were running wild across our country when the Doctor lived…

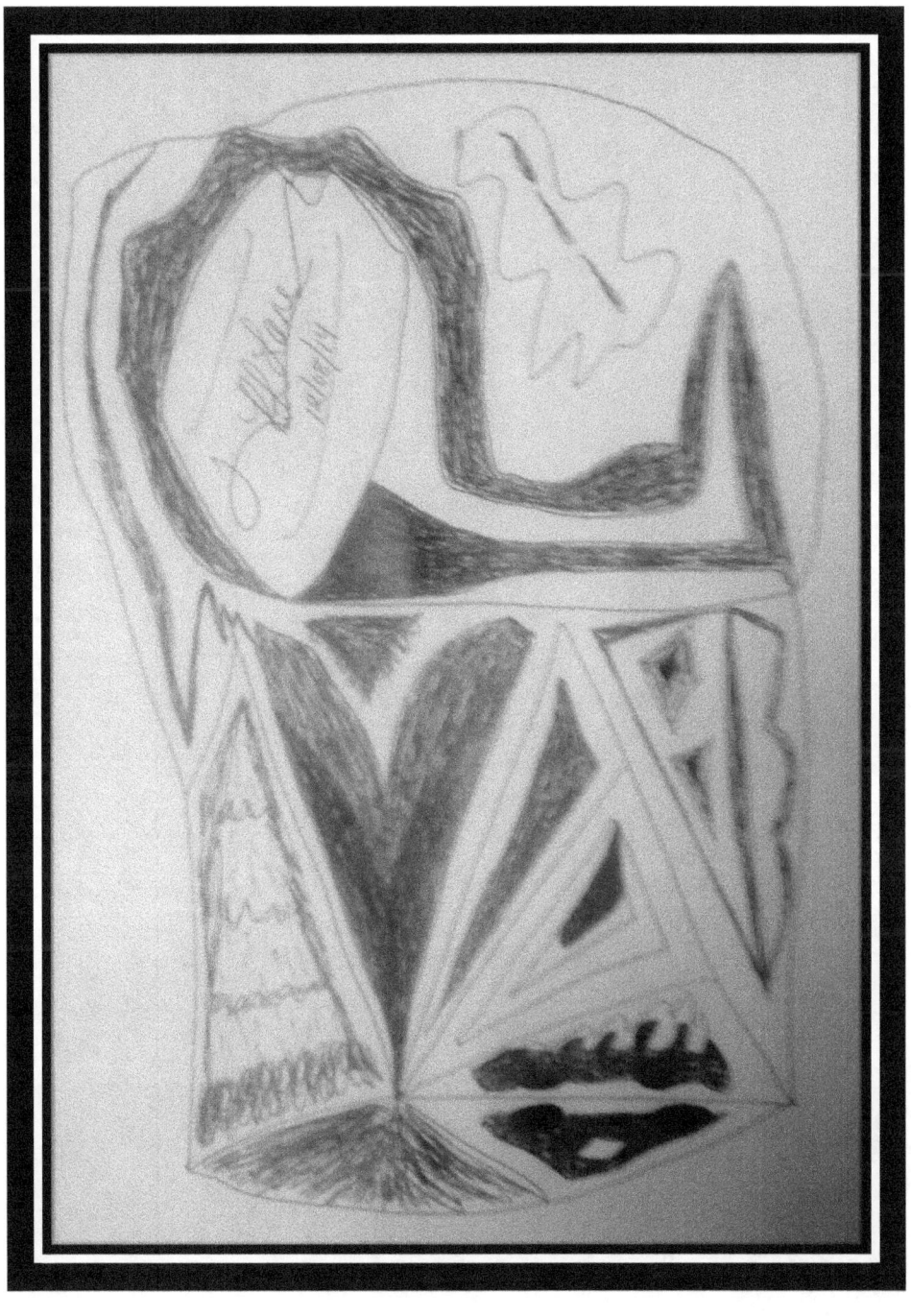

Back in 1940, there was a famous train wreck…the Doctor was the rail surgeon in the nearby small town. He, along with many others, rushed to help…

You had to have a lot of faith to have been a doctor in that generation. The early 1900s…

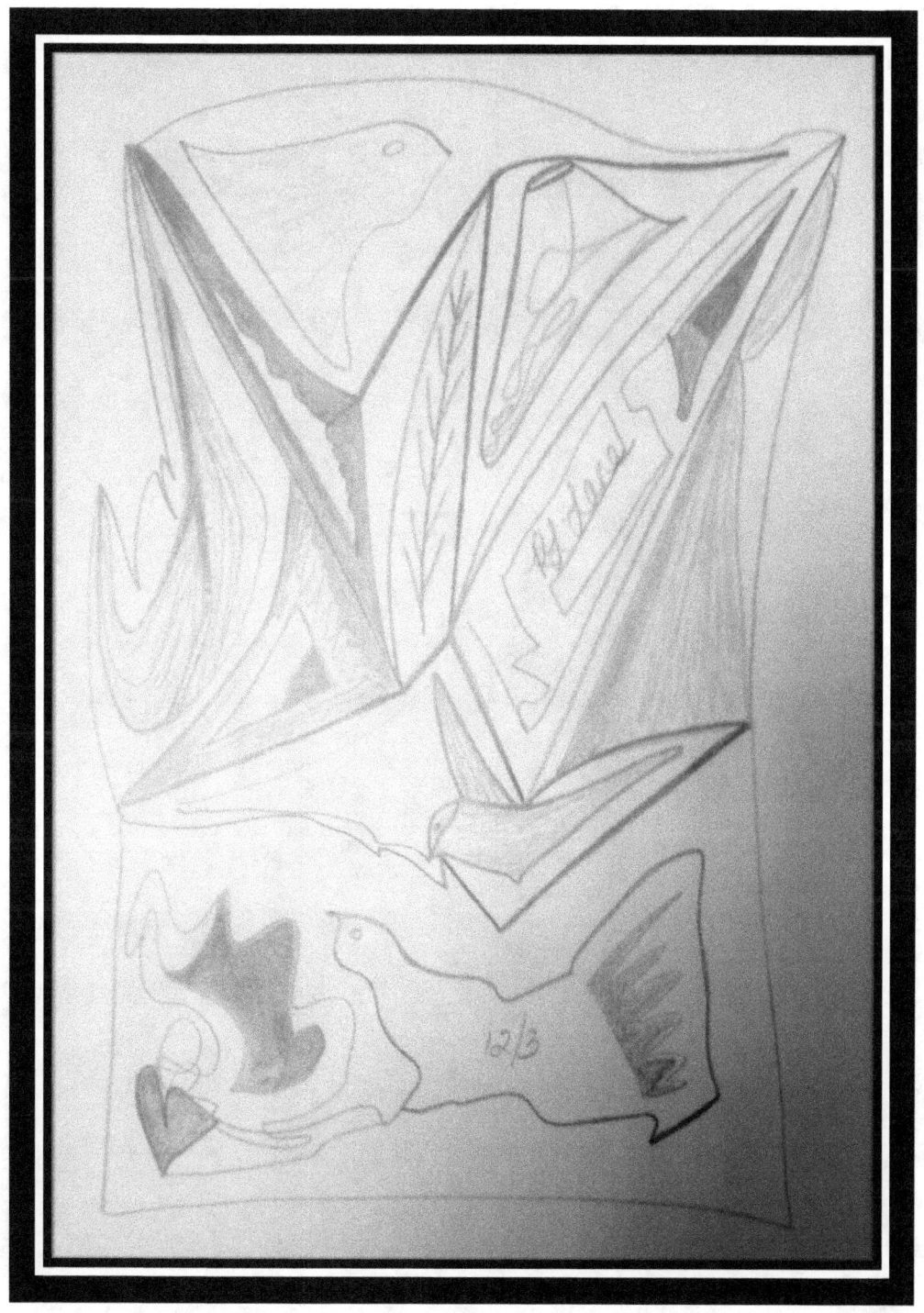

There were big families…they all needed help. They were the key…

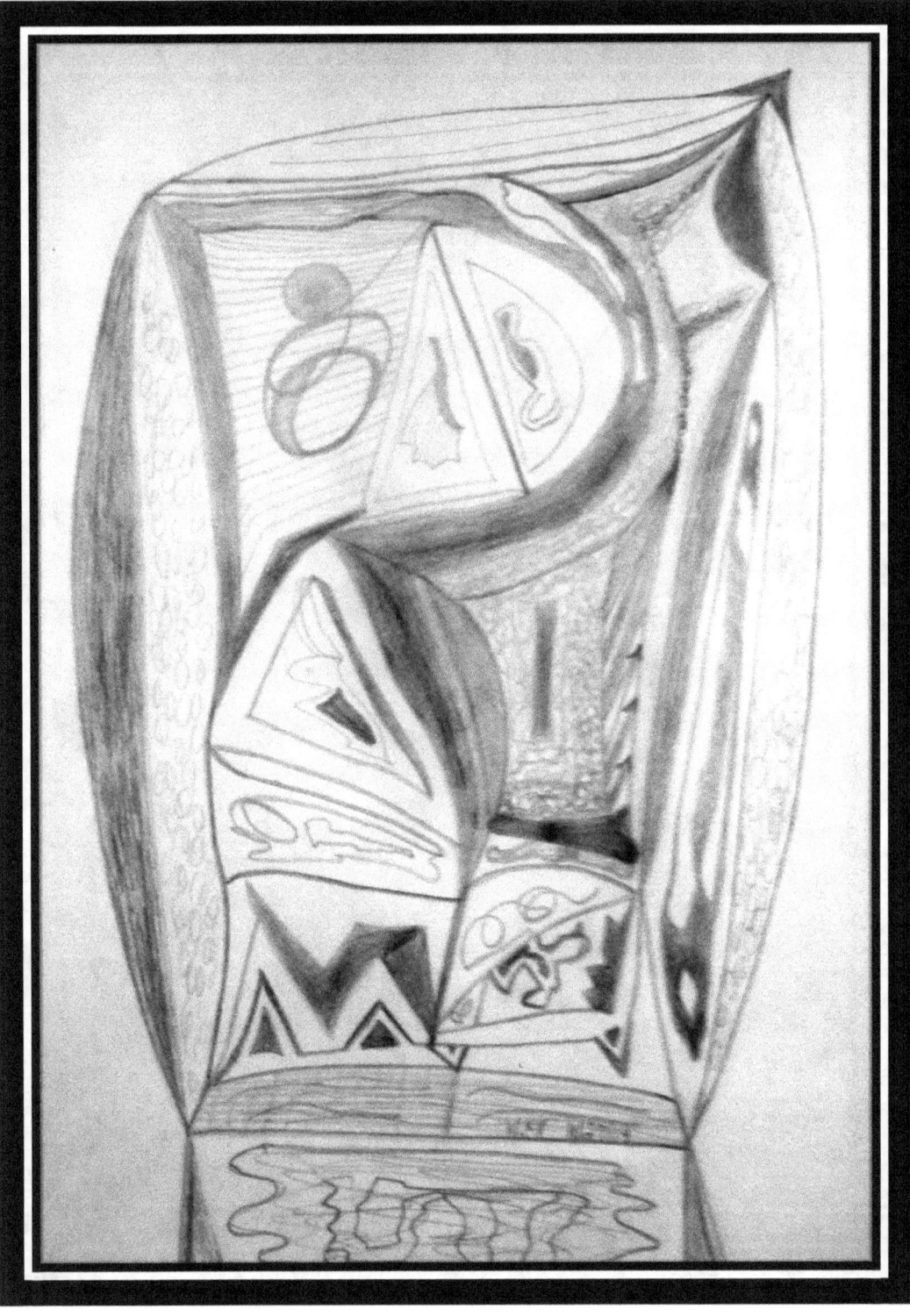

He was Italian. I called this "Pasta Disaster". Well, it would be a disaster if you were Italian and could not make pasta…or if you married an Italian man and could not make pasta…

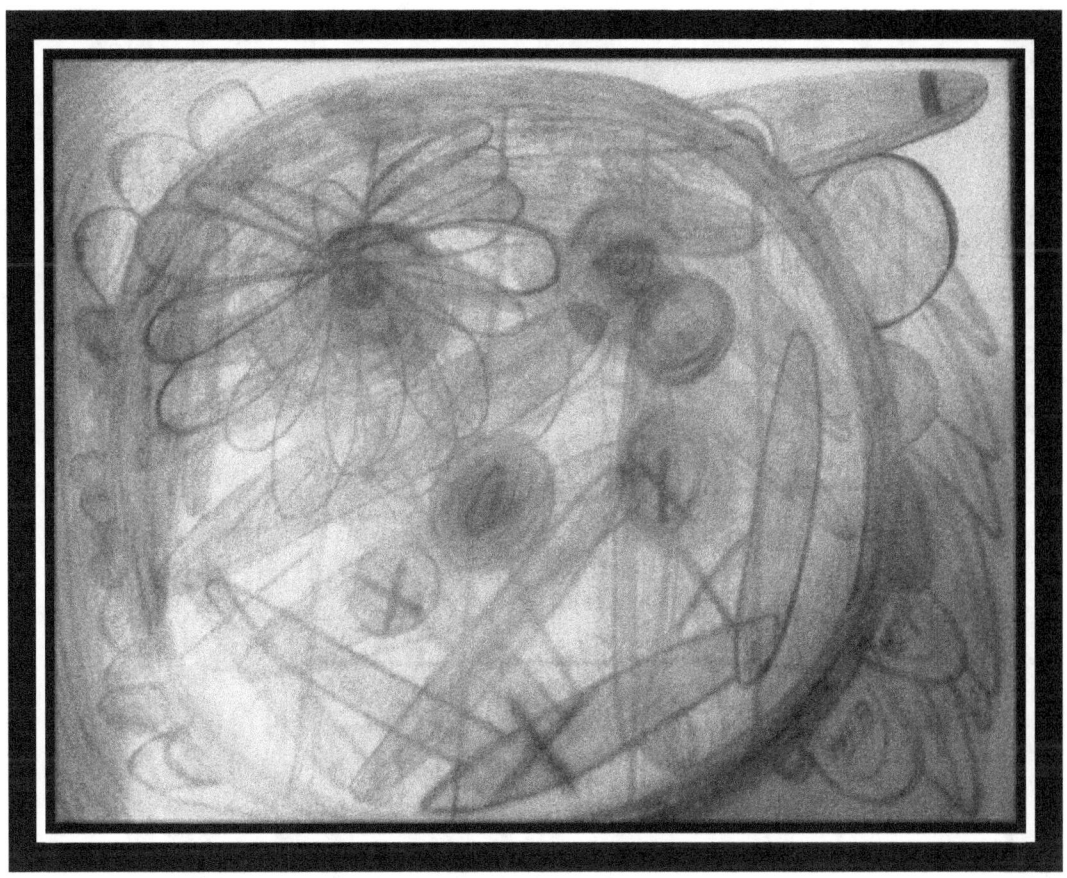

I am still confused by this one. My Santa did not need a deer to light his way. He has a headlamp coming out of the side of his head. *That symbol on the lampshade means something…*

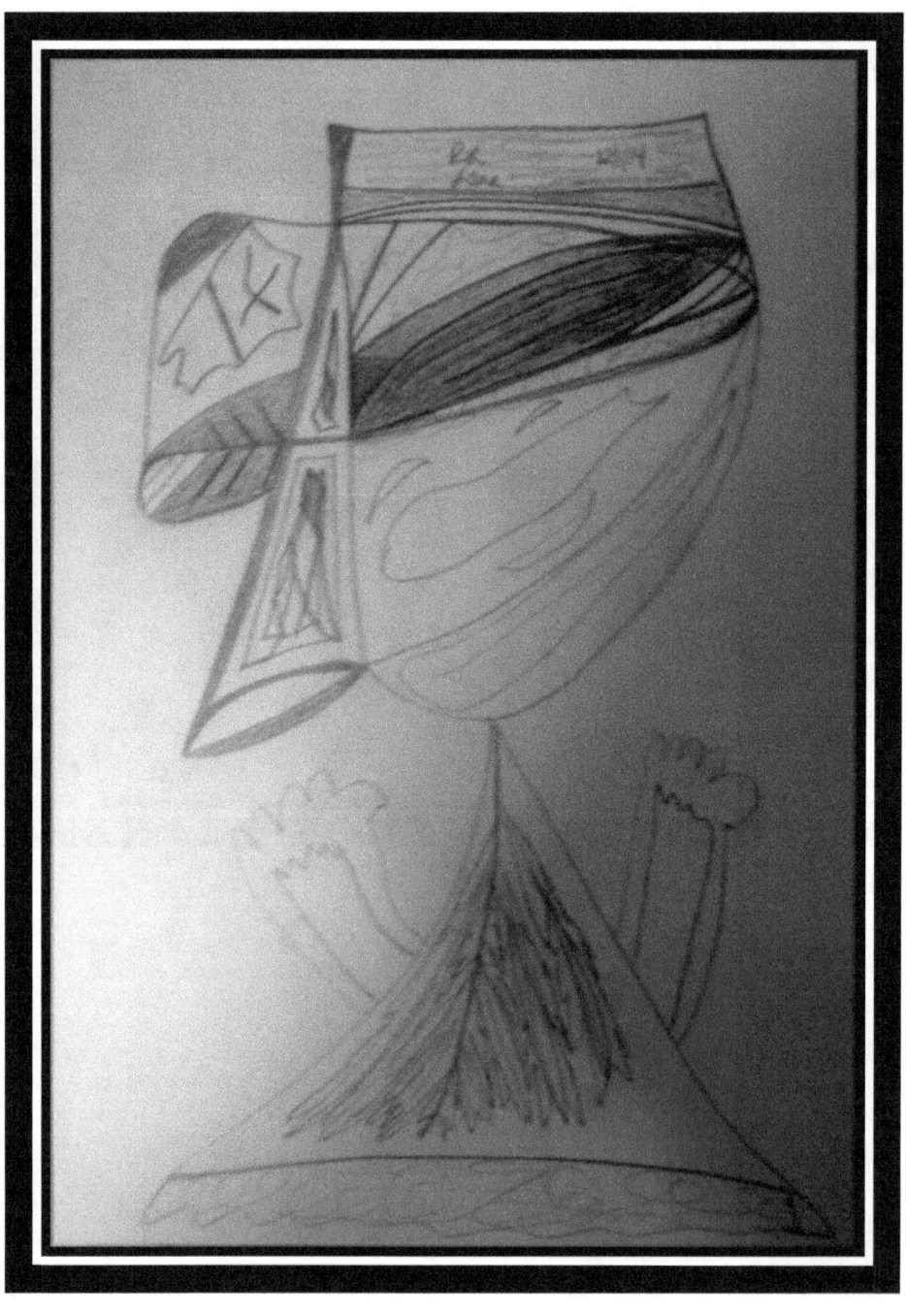

I thought this drawing was "Under Water", and then someone helped me realize it was "Under Ground". That story gets told later…

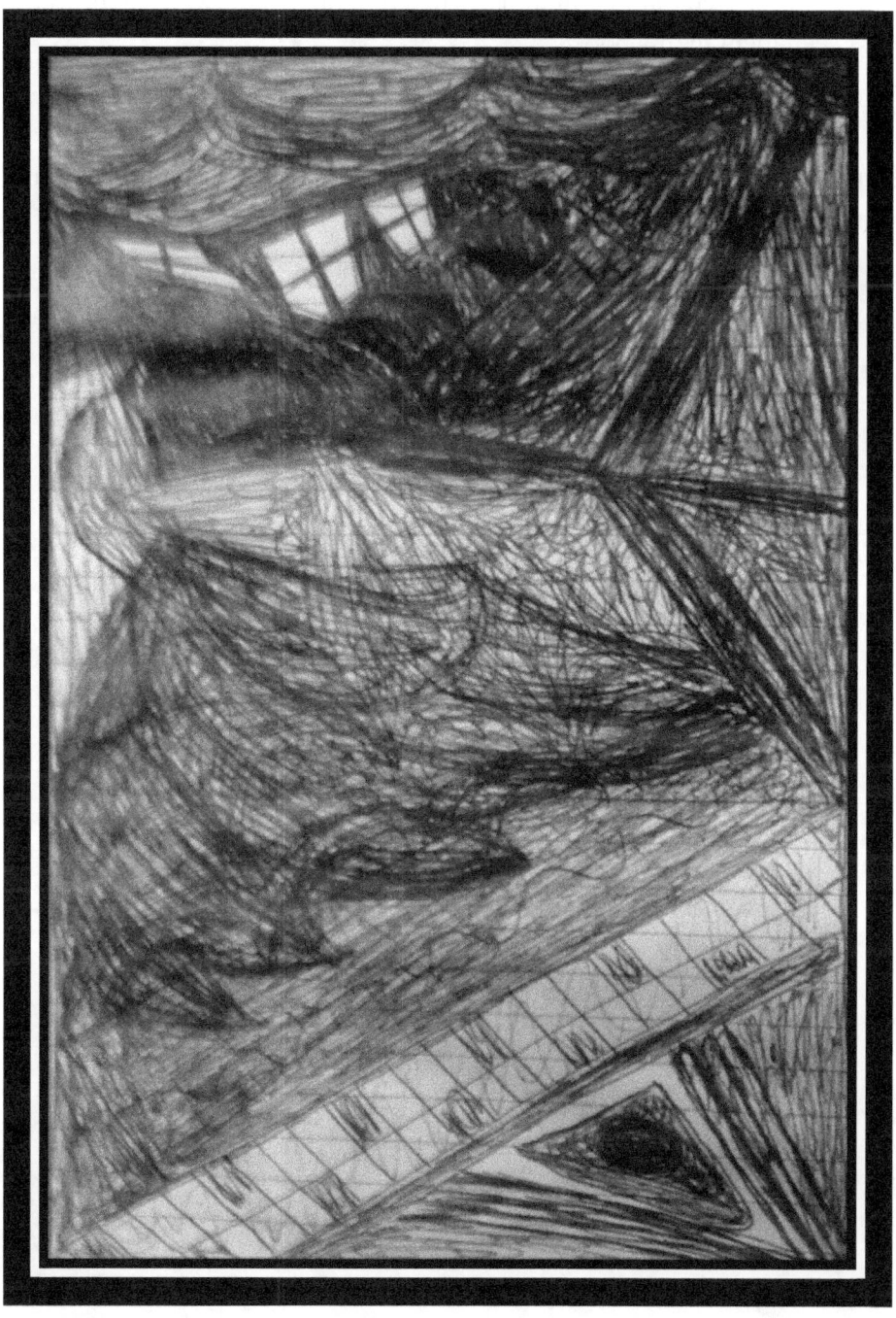

I don't know how I got the light to shine out of the window…it just happened…

I didn't even really realize how he happened. He just did. Then "Chapel Street Signs" was born. The first book of the EcarreT series. The first 3 books of 206,000 words poured out in 6 months. Then the trapped drawings appeared. You have just seen them in this book.

Some of the drawings of "Chapel Street Signs". By RL Lane.

I still haven't seen his face. I will never meet him while I am on the rock, but I drew him on his ship. USS LST 494 in active combat during WWII...

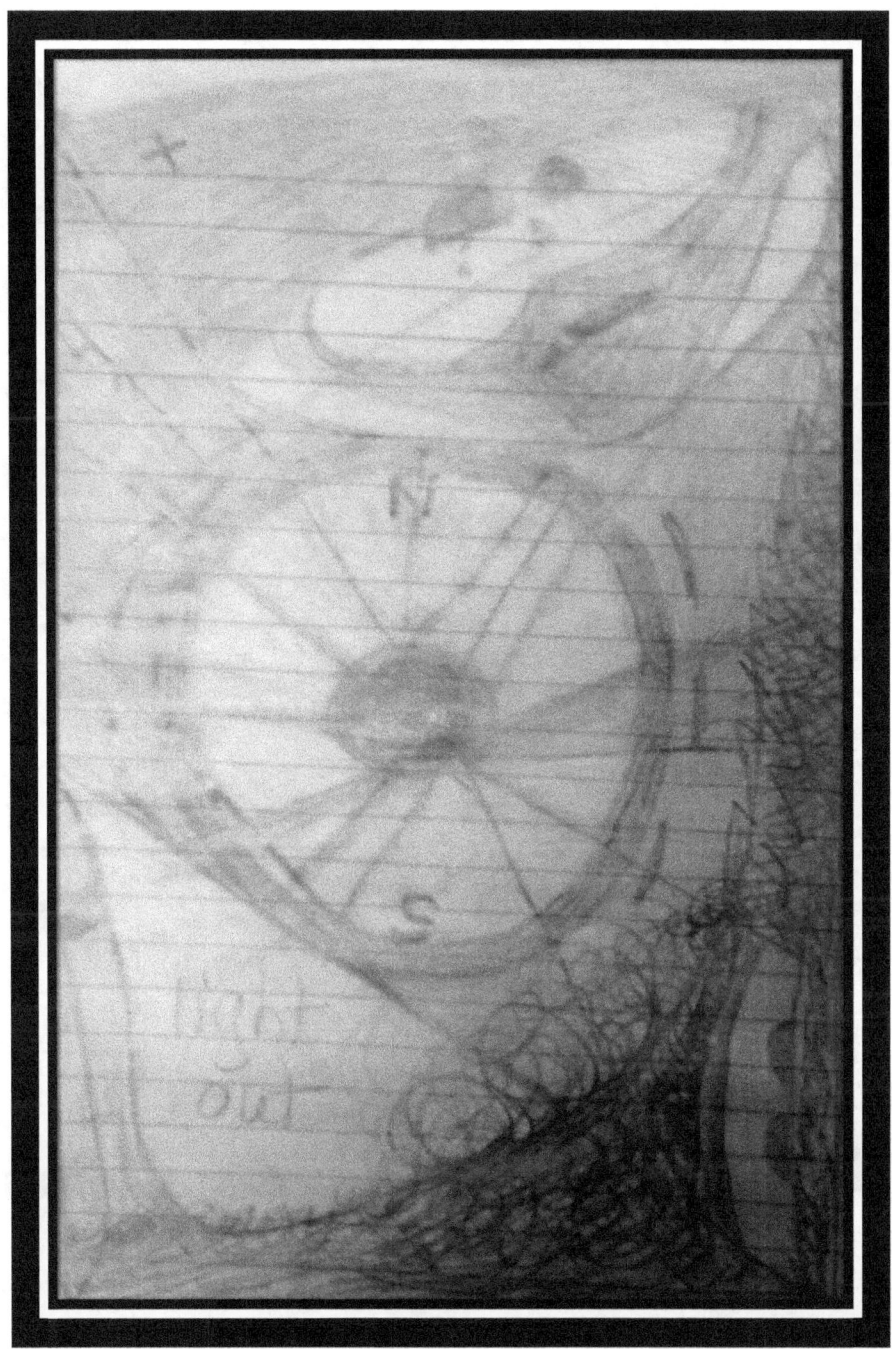

He says the wheel on his ship was 12 feet long. It doesn't seem possible, but that is what he said. I hope someone with access to the Navy ship archives can help me one day prove that his message is right…

I hope we can figure it out before I walk into the…

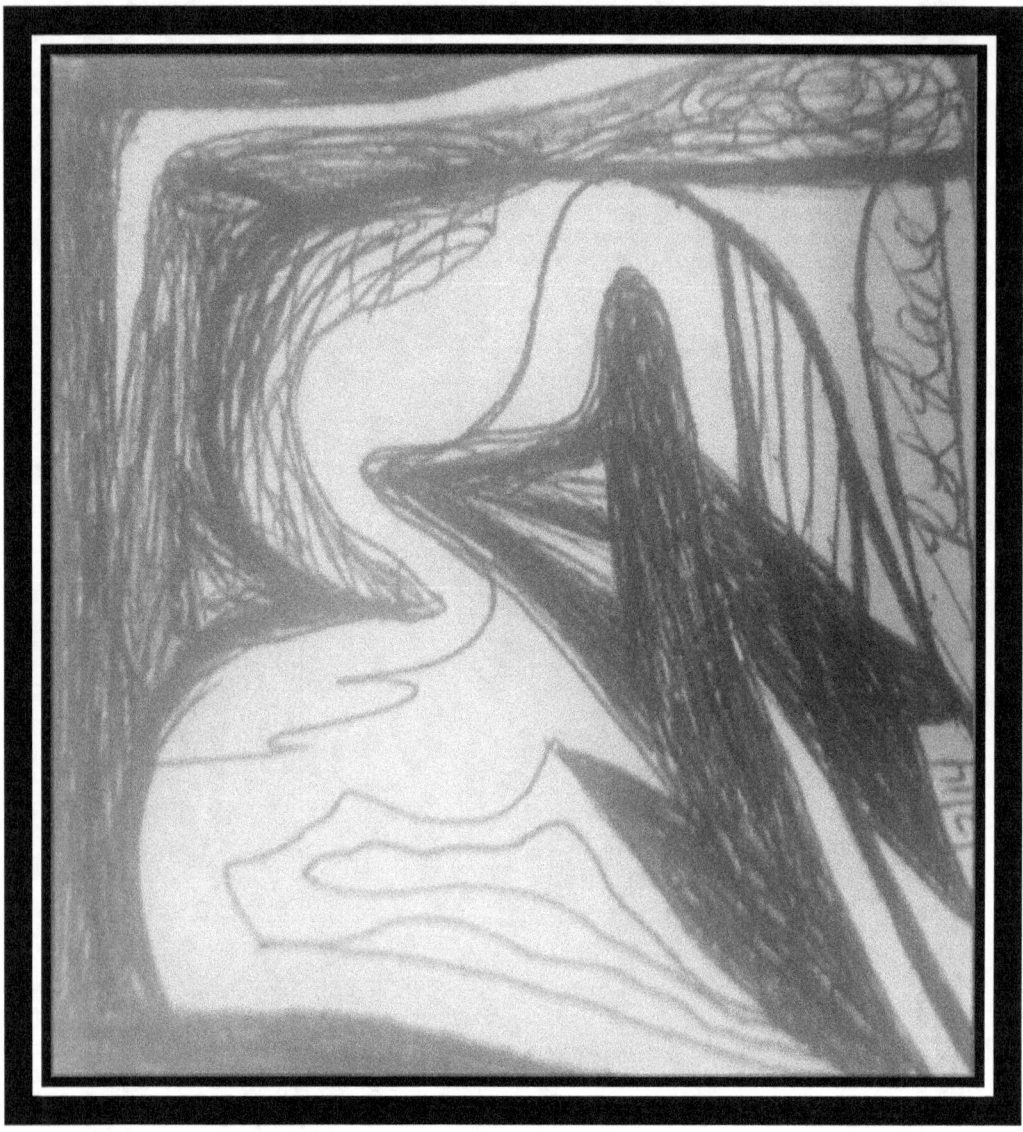

Turn it around, and you'll see all the letters of LOVE.

Love,

RL Lane

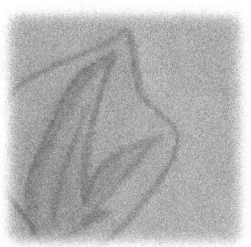